PAT LOWE

THE GIRL WITH NO NAME

Edited by: Britt-Katrin Keson
Illustrated by: Peter Bay-Alexandersen

EASY READERS
ER
EASY READERS

The vocabulary is based on
Michael West: A General Service List of
English Words, revised & enlarged edition 1953
Pacemaker Core Vocabulary, 1975
Salling/Hvid: English-Danish Basic Dictionary, 1970
J. A. van Ek: The Threshold Level for Modern Language
Learning in Schools, 1976

Series editors:
Ulla Malmmose and Charlotte Bistrup

Cover illustration: Peter Bay-Alexandersen
Cover layout: Mette Plesner

First published by Penguin Books Australia, 1994

- a subsidiary of Lindhardt og Ringhof Forlag A/S,
an Egmont company.
ISBN Denmark 978-87-23-90258-0
www.easyreaders.eu
The CEFR levels stated on the back of the book
are approximate levels.

Easy Readers
EGMONT

Printed in Denmark

Pat Lowe was born in the UK in 1941. In 1972 she emigrated to Australia, where she worked as a psychologist in Western Australian prisons. In addition to *The Girl with No Name* (1994), Pat Lowe has also written *Jilji – Life in the Great Sandy Desert* (1990) and *Yinti – Desert Child* (1992). Both these books were written with, and illustrated by, Jimmy Pike, an Aboriginal artist from the Great Sandy Desert. In 1998 she wrote *The Boab Tree* about the remarkable tree that traditionally has been very important to Aboriginal Australians.

Timor Sea
Darwin
INDIAN OCEAN
Kimberley
Northern Territory
Queens-land
Great Barrier Reef
PACIFIC OCEAN
Great Sandy Desert.
Alice Springs
Western Australia
Brisbane
South Australia
Meekatharra
New South Wales
Newcastle
Sydney
Perth
Victoria
Canberra
Adelaide
Melbourne
INDIAN OCEAN
Hobart
Tasmania

Chapter 1 – Lost

Matthew stood on the top of the rocky hill and looked out in the direction he thought he had come from. He saw red earth, rock, green grass, a few short trees and bushes. He felt the warm sun on his skin, and the light wind that dried the *sweat* on his neck. He heard the sound of a bird calling. In his stomach he felt fear. He was lost.

Matthew had left his home early that morning, even before his mother was up. He had taken his bicycle, his *sleeping-bag* and a *backpack* containing food and a bottle of water. It was rare in the far north of the country for the weather to be cool enough for cycling long distances. Matthew had promised himself a trip during the July school holidays. At this time of year he could count on warm, fine days, cool nights and early mornings. 'I'll go tomorrow,' he had told his mother the previous evening.

Earlier in the holidays, Matthew and his parents had been through the question of whether or not he was old enough to go camping out alone. His father had taken his side. 'He's not a kid any more,' he had said. 'I left home and got my first job when I was not much older than he is.'

'What if anything happens to him?'

'He's as safe out there as he is riding to school every day. You can't keep an eye on him forever.'

'The *Kimberley*'s not like Perth,' Matthew said.

sweat, [swet] salty liquid given off by the body through the skin
sleeping-bag, backpack, see picture, pages 6/7
Kimberley, region in the far north of Western Australia

'There's not much traffic, and the only people likely to be around are locals or tourists. Lots of kids from my class go camping without their parents.'

'Not on their own,' said his mother.

'It's an *adventure*,' said Matthew. 'I've always wanted to see what it's like to sleep by myself in the *bush*. Goanna G*orge* is only about thirty kilometres away – it's not as if I'm going miles out into the *desert* or something. It's just for one night, and you'll know exactly where I am.'

'He's a *sensible* kid,' his father added, looking at his son. 'We want him to be independent.'

In the end, Matthew's mother had given in.

adventure, exciting and often dangerous journey
bush, wild land with bushes and trees (esp. in Australia or Africa)
gorge, [gɔːdʒ] deep, narrow valley made by a small river running through it
desert, ['dezət] large area of land with very little rain and few plants
sensible, having good sense or practical wisdom, reasonable

'I'll ride out as far as Goanna Gorge and camp there. I can drink from the *pool*, and refill my water-bottle for the ride back.'

'What time will you be home?' his mother asked.

Matthew put his arm around her. 'No later than sunset,' he had promised.

The ride to Goanna Gorge on his new mountain bike seemed longer than Matthew had expected. The morning air was cool, but he soon began to sweat. The sun rose above the hills as he went. He liked the sense of freedom as he cycled down the empty road.

Later, Matthew passed a couple of cars pulling *caravans*. The drivers waved at him, and he lifted a hand in

pool, small area of still water, waterhole

reply. At heart, he hated tourists. He tried to *remind* himself that they were only out trying to enjoy themselves. But it always seemed pointless to him – driving from one place to another simply to look at it. When he was old enough to travel, Matthew decided, he would only go to places *off the beaten track*. He would always travel with a purpose, for the sake of real adventure.

Today's trip had a special purpose, besides the bike ride and the adventure of camping out alone. Matthew had heard that there were rock paintings somewhere in Goanna Gorge. His father, who was an officer at the local *prison*, had been told about them by one of the prisoners. The man had described the place to find them: near the pool and across from a particular *boab tree*. Matthew had said nothing to his father at the time, but he had made up his mind to find the paintings one day.

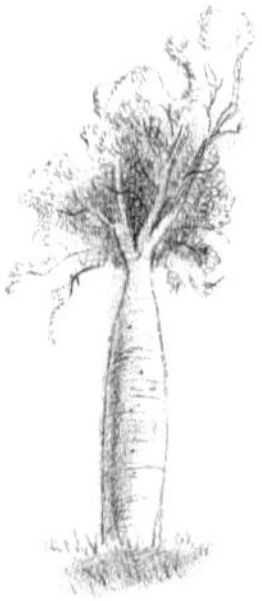

boab tree

remind, cause to remember or think of
off the beaten track, not often visited by people
prison, large building in which people who have committed crimes are kept as a punishment
boab tree, ['bəʊˌæb 'triː] tree with a very thick trunk that grows in Australia

By the time he reached the top of Goanna Gorge, Matthew was ready for a rest. He left his bike by a tree, slipped the backpack off his shoulders, took out his water-bottle and had a long drink. He stood for a moment at the edge of the gorge, looking down into the valley below. Then he carried his backpack and sleeping-bag down into the gorge and hid them behind some bushes beside the pool.

Matthew filled his water-bottle with water from the pool and started off down the valley. As he walked between the large rocks, he kept his eye on the western side of the valley, looking for the paintings. From time to time he looked over at the eastern side, hoping to recognise the boab tree.

When Matthew had listened to his father's description of the place, he had seen in his mind's eye the side of the valley and the boab tree. He had felt sure he would recognise the tree as soon as he saw it. Now that he was down in the valley itself, the scene was quite different. There were boab trees here and there all through the valley. How could he possibly know which was the right one?

After perhaps an hour of walking, Matthew noticed that he was coming to the end of the valley. He must have missed the place he was looking for. He sat on a rock and looked back up the gorge in the direction of the pool. 'If I wanted to make a rock painting,' he said to himself, 'where would I do it?' This thought made it clear to him how little he knew about *Aboriginal* people. I wonder if they'd have gone for the easiest place?

Aboriginal, [ˌæbəˈrɪdʒənəl] living in Australia from the earliest times (before the arrival of white people)

he thought. What were they painting for, anyway? They might have wanted their paintings to be hidden, not out in the open where everyone could see them.

Suddenly he felt sure that he could see the answer. Some way back and across the valley the rock was like a flat wall. It's a natural gallery! thought Matthew. He turned and looked across the valley to the other side. There was a tall young boab tree. Matthew climbed over the loose rocks and reached the wall. At first he saw nothing. Then, suddenly, in front of him, in the same colours as the rock itself, were the paintings. 'I've found them!' he said aloud. Although he knew that other white people must have been there before him, he imagined himself the first *explorer* ever to have stood there.

The red and white paintings covered most of the wall. Matthew could see the shapes of individual figures, including several figures he knew from books. There was a pair of reptiles that might have been crocodiles or perhaps *lizards*. There was also a series of smaller figures, and he saw the outline of a hand held flat against the rock, like the artist's *signature*.

When he was sure he had seen all the paintings there were to be seen, Matthew sat for a while and thought about them. How old were the paintings? He tried to imagine who the artists were, and what their lives might have been like. They had been right here, where he was sitting now. He could almost feel their presence. Matthew imagined the artists as young men

explorer, person who travels to unknown areas for the purpose of discovery
lizard, small reptile with four legs and a long tail
signature, ['sɪgnətʃə] person's name written by him/herself

wearing *headbands*, such as he had seen in books. They had left their *spears* leaning nearby against the rock while they worked. He could imagine older men with grey *beards* watching them. Or maybe the old men were the painters, Matthew thought now. They could have been using the rock like a blackboard, to teach important stories to the younger people. Some of the paintings were old, but others looked as if they had been painted recently. How long ago? Matthew wondered. It could have been in the last year or two. Maybe people still came here to do that. He looked back over his shoulder, almost expecting to see dark figures coming down the valley towards him. Suddenly he felt

spear, [spɪə] stick with a sharp point used for hunting, etc.
beard, [bɪəd] hair on a man's face

like a *trespasser*. With the strange feeling that someone might be watching him, he got up. He took one last look at the paintings, and then he turned to go.

Once he had left the valley and the rock paintings behind, Matthew headed at once for the nearest hill. Maybe he'd find more paintings. He'd be the first white person to find them. Matthew wondered what he'd do. He imagined his photo in the local paper, under the headline: 'Schoolboy makes important discovery'. He'd be standing in front of the previously unknown rock paintings, surrounded by *reporters*, even television cameras. No, that wasn't such a good idea. He wouldn't mind being famous, but he couldn't bear the thought of all those people coming out to this wild place. And it wouldn't stop there. The paintings might become a tourist attraction. The whole place would be ruined. No, it would be better to keep the paintings a secret.

The hill was further away than it had looked. When he reached it, he could see that there was nowhere for an artist to paint. The entire hill was covered with broken rocks. Matthew climbed to the top and looked about him. For as far as he could see in any direction, there was no sign of human life. He could not even see the road, hidden as it was somewhere among the hills.

He was surprised that he could no longer see the valley he had just left. Surely it was over there? Matthew came down the hill. At the foot of the hill, nothing looked familiar. He couldn't be sure which was the exact spot where he had started to climb up. He

trespasser, ['trespəsə] person who enters private property or land without the owner's permission
reporter, person who writes about news events, usually for a newspaper

thought it might be here – or was it a little further to the right?

Well, thought Matthew, I'm sure I came out of the valley over there. That must be almost due east. He remembered that he had thought the valley ran roughly north and south. Now he was less certain. He tried to remember the position of the sun as it had shone down into the valley. At this cooler time of year it would still be well to the north. Had the sun been shining straight down the valley at midday? He was *ashamed* that he couldn't properly remember.

Don't start getting *frightened*, he told himself. Just sit down and think. It'll come back. He sat down for a few moments, but he got up again at once. He felt he had to do something. He headed towards what he hoped was the valley. Matthew continued walking in the same direction for a while longer. Suddenly he was certain he had gone too far. It had only taken him about twenty minutes to walk from the valley to the foot of the hill. He seemed to have been going twice as long on the way back.

Matthew remembered his daydream about making an important discovery. No real explorer would get lost, he thought. I didn't even bring my *compass* – what an idiot! He'd been given a compass for his birthday, and had never used it except in fun around the garden for the first day or so.

compass

ashamed, feeling bad or foolish about something
frightened, ['fraɪtənd] full of fear, afraid
compass, ['kʌmpəs] instrument with a needle that points north

Then Matthew made another mistake. Instead of going back towards the hill, he headed off to the left, which he was sure was north. By doing this he lost sight of the hill altogether. Sweating in the afternoon heat, he climbed another hill to try to work out where he was. From the top he could see neither valley nor hill. He no longer had any idea of where he had started out. All he knew was that he was facing east again, with the afternoon sun behind him. Matthew was forced to admit to himself that he was lost.

Chapter 2 – Found

Matthew had found a spot under a rock away from the wind, but he still was cold. The stars were shining above him, and there was no moon. He looked up at the sky and for a moment almost forgot about being lost. He had never before spent a night alone in the bush. He had been camping out a few times, with a group of friends, but that had felt quite different. His main memories of those trips were of the fun he had had with the other boys.

I wish Nick or one of the others was here now, he thought. I'm sure Nick would find something to laugh at. Nick was the joker in the group, and that was one reason Matthew liked him. Whereas Matthew was quiet and thoughtful, Nick was outgoing. Matthew laughed more when he was with Nick than he did with anyone else. To pass the time now he tried to imagine Nick sitting there beside him. When, in a few days' time, Matthew told him about this night, Nick would be sure to *tease* him. 'Captain Matthew Scott the explorer!' he'd say.

On all those trips with the other boys, their camping places had never been this far off the beaten track. They had camped in public caravan parks. There had always been at least a few adults within reach. This was different. It was just Matthew and the bush. If he had not been lost, cold, *hungry* and a bit frightened, he would have enjoyed the adventure.

He didn't doubt he would be found sooner or later. He knew that if he wasn't home tomorrow, his father would have a *search party* out first thing the next morning. His colleagues in the prison service and the police force would join him. So Matthew kept telling himself, but at the back of his mind he couldn't quite get rid of the thought: What if they don't find me in time? What if I run out of water?

If only it wasn't so cold. All he had on was a T-shirt and shorts. Every so often Matthew got up and walked a few steps back and forth near the rock, waving his arms to warm himself up. He wondered what his parents were doing. They were probably asleep. They wouldn't even start worrying about him until tomorrow evening. That seemed ages away.

It was an endless night – the worst night Matthew could ever remember, but at sunrise Matthew started feeling more optimistic. Tomorrow he would be found, he was sure. It was going to be hard to sit and do nothing, waiting for someone to find him, but he knew that would be the safest thing to do. He was afraid of another night like the one he had just been through. I

tease, [tiːz] make jokes about or laugh at
hungry, needing or wanting food
search party, group formed to look for a lost person

could try making fire by *rubbing* two sticks together, he told himself. He had an idea of how it was done, but he didn't know what sort of wood to use. Still, it was worth a try.

Suddenly, Matthew thought he heard a sound that wasn't the wind, or a bird, or a lizard. He sat up and looked around, but couldn't see anything that hadn't been there before. He suddenly felt that someone was watching him. He sat very still, listening. Then he heard a voice quite close by, laughing softly. It was a young voice. He stood up quickly, turned, and looked all around. Again he couldn't see anything. He wondered if he had started hearing things that weren't there. He sat down again, looked up, and found himself looking into an upside-down face. It was a black face with a wide smile showing white teeth. Then the face was gone.

'Hey!' shouted Matthew, jumping up. A figure climbed down to the ground a few yards away. It was a girl.

'Hello!' said Matthew. 'Where did you come from?'

The girl looked at him without answering, still smiling. She was younger than Matthew.

'What's your name?' Matthew tried again.

'I know your name,' said the girl. 'You're Matthew Scott.'

'How do you know that?' Matthew was surprised.

The girl *shrugged*. 'Everybody knows you. Your father works at the prison.' The girl spoke English with an accent, as if she were not speaking her own language.

rub, move back and forth against each other
shrug, lift one's shoulders, usually to show that one doesn't know or care about something

'That's right, he does. How come I don't know you?' Even as he said this, Matthew realised he already knew the answer. The only black kids he knew were the ones in his own class at school. But the girl just shrugged again.

'Where did you come from?' Matthew asked a second time. 'Do you know the way back to Goanna Gorge? I got lost yesterday.'

The girl laughed the same soft laugh Matthew had heard before. 'Of course I know,' she said.

'I've been here all night.'

The girl *nodded*. 'I know. I saw your *tracks*.'

'What are you doing out here?'

'My family has got a camp not far from here. Me, I'm going hunting.'

'Really? Do girls go hunting?' Matthew was surprised.

She laughed again. 'Of course we go hunting. We've got to get meat!'

'What sort of animals do you hunt?'

'Oh, *goannas*, snakes, cats – any kind.' She looked around. 'Where did you sleep?'

'Right here.' Matthew showed her. 'It was cold, I can tell you.'

'Why didn't you light a fire?'

goanna

nod, bend one's head down, usually to show that one agrees
track, mark left by a person, animal, etc. in passing along
goanna, [gəʊ'ænə] large lizard with a long tail that lives in Australia

'No *matches*. I left them behind with my other things at Goanna Gorge, near the pool.'

'There are plenty of bush matches,' said the girl, pointing to a small tree not far from where they were standing.

'Bush matches? Oh, you mean you know how to make a fire from sticks?' asked Matthew.

'Of course. A *blackfeller* has got to know.'

'Well, I wish you'd show me. I've never seen anyone make a fire from sticks. If you show me, I'll be able to do it next time I run out of matches.'

She looked at him for another moment without saying anything, then seemed to make up her mind. She went to the tree and broke off a couple of straight dead *branches*, only about half a centimetre thick. She broke off the ends, and then pulled up some dry grass. She picked up a couple of rocks and sat on the ground with her legs crossed. Then she beat the grass with the rock.

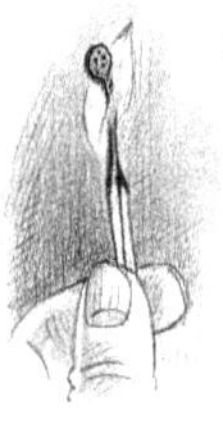

match

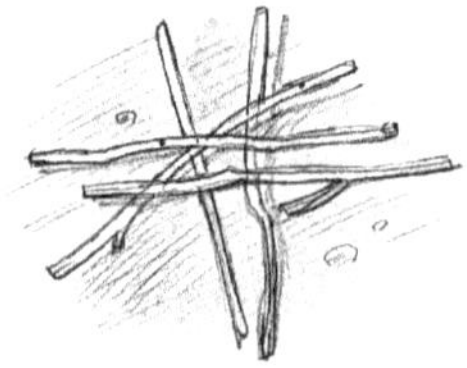

branches

'Why are you doing that?' asked Matthew.

'To make it soft,' said the girl, 'so it can burn.' With the edge of a piece of stone she made a little hole in the side of one of the sticks, and *sharpened* one end of the

blackfeller, (=black fellow) Aboriginal person (not a polite word)
sharpen, make sharp or pointed

other stick. Then she placed the stick with the hole flat on the grass. She placed the second stick upright with the sharpened end in the hole. She held the upright stick between both hands.

'I might not be able to light it,' she said, looking up at Matthew. 'We don't do it much.'

'Why's that?'

'Because we have got the other kind of matches!' she laughed.

Matthew watched while the girl *twirled* the upright stick back and forth between her hands. After a while, smoke rose from between the two sticks. The girl stopped and blew into the dry grass under the sticks. She shook her head. 'No good,' she said.

'Let me have a go,' said Matthew. He sat in front of the girl with his legs crossed, and twirled the upright stick as she had done. But he found it was much harder than it looked. There wasn't the least sign of smoke.

'Never mind,' said the girl. 'You can do it next time.'

Matthew put the sticks carefully into the pocket of his T-shirt. 'You still haven't told me your name,' he said to the girl.

She looked down and seemed *embarrassed*. 'I've got no name,' she said at last.

Matthew couldn't believe it. 'You must have a name. Everyone has a name.'

The girl shook her head. 'A woman passed away. She had the same name as me.'

'You mean people can't use that name any more?'

twirl, [twɜːl] turn round and round quickly
embarrassed, [ɪmˈbærəst] feeling bad or uncomfortable about the situation

Matthew asked. He remembered hearing about the *custom* of changing names that were the same as that of a dead person. 'So what do people call you now?'

'Kumunyjayi,' said the girl after a pause. 'That means "no name".'

'No name,' said Matthew thoughtfully. 'That's what I'll call you: No-name.'

No-name laughed.

'Are we far from Goanna Gorge?' he asked No-name.

'Not too far,' she said. 'You want me to show you?'

'Yeah, I wish you would. I left all my things there, and if I don't go home today my parents will have a search party out looking for me.'

No-name nodded. She stood up and Matthew got up, too. To Matthew's surprise, she did not lead him back the way he had come, but cut across country.

'Is Goanna Gorge this way?' he asked.

'Yeah.' The girl pointed. 'That way.'

Matthew looked hard in the direction she was pointing, but could see nothing special about that part of the landscape. He wondered how she knew. She seemed so sure of herself, he did not for a moment doubt her. He simply followed.

custom, common practice or behaviour in a social group

Chapter 3 – No-name

The girl led him in a more or less straight line. Once, she stopped to *examine* some tracks in the sand at her feet. Matthew came alongside and looked down.

'Goanna, fresh tracks,' said No-name, and set off walking fast after the tracks. Matthew followed. Suddenly the girl started to run, and Matthew saw the goanna running fast through the grass. No-name was after it, and Matthew found it hard to keep up. The girl fell to her knees and started digging fast with her hands at a hole in the ground. In a few moments she pulled the goanna backwards from the hole by its tail and held it up for Matthew to see. Then she beat the animal's head twice against the ground. She examined it to make sure it was dead, then handed it to Matthew. He took it. Its head was bloody, its eyes closed, and its long *tongue* was hanging out.

'You like eating goanna?'

'Never tried it,' said Matthew. 'What's it like?'

'Good meat,' said No-name, standing up. She started off again. Matthew walked along behind, carrying the goanna by its tail.

At one little hill, No-name pointed over to the right. 'My camp is that way,' she said. 'You want to look?'

'Why not?' Now that Matthew knew he was safe, he didn't need to hurry back. He felt *curious* about his new friend's life, and wanted to learn more about her.

No-name led Matthew off to the right, where she

examine, [ɪg'zæmɪn] look at carefully in order to find out something
tongue, [tʌŋ] movable organ in the mouth used for tasting food, etc.
curious, ['kjʊərɪəs] wanting to know or find out something

had pointed. Some distance away there were trees at the foot of a low hill. As they approached the trees Matthew noticed an old *truck* parked under one of them. Smoke rose nearby from a fire he couldn't see yet. A woman carrying a metal *bucket* walked in the direction of the smoke. No-name called out to her: 'Eh!' The woman stopped in her tracks and looked towards them.

'My grandmother,' the girl told Matthew.

They walked to the elderly woman, who seemed not at all surprised to see them. She put her bucket, half-full of water, on the fire and straightened up.

'This is Matthew,' said No-name. The woman smiled

and nodded as if she already knew him.

'Is he Jampijin?' the old woman asked, smiling at her granddaughter, who laughed and shook her head. Matthew smiled and waited for No-name to explain the joke, but she didn't.

'You got lost,' the old woman said to Matthew.

'How did you know?' he asked.

'We saw your tracks all round, last night,' said the woman. 'Up and down, up and down you went.' She laughed. 'But it was too late to look for you. We couldn't find you at night. We waited until the morning. My granddaughter was worried for you. She went off early to look for you. And she found you all right.'

She laughed again.

So the girl had come especially looking for him. Matthew was beginning to understand that to people like No-name and her grandmother, the idea of getting lost in the bush was funny. They laughed at him as he might laugh at someone of his own age who didn't know how to ride a bike. He had seen how easily No-name made her way through the countryside. Maybe it's the same as me knowing my way around Perth, thought Matthew. I was brought up there, and I suppose they've spent all their lives around here.

His father had been *transferred* north two years before. Even though people who moved north led more of an outdoors life, they still lived in town. They only went into the bush now and then, usually on long weekends, to well-known fishing and camping spots.

Meanwhile, No-name had cleaned the dead goanna, and was passing its body through the fire. When the wood was reduced to *charcoal*, No-name used a stick to dig a hole at one side of it. With the same stick she rolled some of the red-hot charcoal into the bottom of the hole, and then laid the goanna on top of it. She covered the goanna with more charcoal and hot sand until there was nothing to see but the tip of the goanna's tail sticking out at one end.

The water in the bucket came to the boil, and the old woman poured a pile of tea-leaves into the bucket. While the tea was being prepared, Matthew looked around the camp. 'Do you live here?' he asked No-name.

'Not all the time,' she told him. 'Only weekends and

transfer, [træns'fɜː] move from one job or place to another
charcoal, wood that has completely burned but still glows red hot

holiday time. My grandmother has got a house in town, too.'

'Whereabouts?' asked Matthew.

'Piyirnwarnti. You know – Two-mile.'

Suddenly Matthew was embarrassed. Two-mile was one of the two small communities that used to be called reserves. Some people still used the old term, because for white people the community names were too hard to *pronounce*. The communities were places Matthew had always, without fully realising it, *looked down on*. He had never actually set foot inside either of them. He had sometimes ridden past them on his bike. He had seen broken-down cars and old houses with fires burning in the front yards, and people sitting outside on the ground. The house he lived in was much bigger, cleaner and neater than any of the houses at the reserve looked from the outside.

Until this moment Matthew had looked on the people in the communities as completely different from himself. If they lived in poor conditions that must be how they wanted it. He had heard adults, his own parents among them, talking about the way Aboriginal people behaved, and how few of them held a job. Never before had he thought of the people in Two-mile as ordinary people much like himself. Nor had it crossed his mind that they might have another side to their lives than sitting in the reserve or hanging around town.

'Are you two here on your own?' he asked.

pronounce, [prə'naʊns] make the sound of (a word, etc.)
look down on, believe that (someone or something) is not as good as oneself

'No. My mother is here, too, and my family, but they have gone walkabout.'

'Walkabout?' said Matthew.

'Yeah, you know – hunting.'

'Why were you walking around yourself?' asked No-name's grandmother suddenly. 'Where is your family?'

'My family? They're at home. I wanted to camp out by myself.' Matthew *hesitated* before adding, 'And I wanted to look for some rock paintings.'

'Blackfeller paintings? You found them?'

Matthew was glad the old woman wasn't angry. On the contrary, she seemed pleased. 'Yes,' he told her. 'I found them on a flat rock, like a wall. Do you know much about them?'

'Very old, those paintings,' said the old woman. 'They tell a very old story.'

'What kind of story?' Matthew was interested.

'An old story, from before people walked round here. You know that kind of story?'

'I think so,' Matthew said. 'You mean stories about how things were made? Animals and everything?'

'That's right. In the early days people painted stories on rock. Those paintings are still there today.'

'Some of the paintings look new. The paint looks fresh.'

'Yeah, that's right,' the old woman said. 'When they get old, people renew them, keep them nice.'

Matthew imagined generation after generation of artists maintaining the records of traditional stories. He tried to think of something similar from his own experience. School teaching? He supposed that was similar.

hesitate, ['hezɪteɪt] pause before doing something

Generations of school teachers passed on the same rules of maths, say, to class after class of students.

After a while, No-name took hold of the goanna's tail and pulled it out of the hole. She broke off the tail and handed it to Matthew.

'You had goanna before?' asked the old woman. Matthew shook his head, looking at the tail.

'It's a good one,' No-name told him. 'You try it.'

Not wanting to be a *wimp*, Matthew took hold of a piece of the tail and pulled. The meat looked like a piece of chicken. He put it into his mouth, and to his surprise the meat tasted good.

'Good one?' asked No-name, smiling. Matthew nodded, and she and her grandmother laughed.

When they had finished the goanna and the tea, No-name started telling her grandmother the story of how she found Matthew. She spoke fast in a dialect that seemed to be mostly English, but Matthew did not understand very much.

Matthew was beginning to wonder if No-name had forgotten about taking him back to Goanna Gorge. Perhaps she thought he should be able to find his own way from here.

'I'd better start heading back, now,' he said. 'Can you show me the way?' he asked No-name, but she was already on her feet.

'The waterhole is not too far,' she told him.

Again the girl seemed to know exactly which way to go. No-name didn't seem to be hurrying, but Matthew found himself walking fast to keep up with her. He felt a bit silly following the girl's footprints so closely, but

wimp, weak or useless person, coward

she always picked the easiest way through the bush.

The sun was hotter, but there was still a cool east wind blowing, and Matthew didn't sweat much. He kept thinking about the previous night. He wondered how he would be feeling now if No-name had not come looking for him. Instead of having to wait for a search party to find him, Matthew would now be able to go home at the expected time. His parents need not even know that anything had gone wrong.

Maybe I shouldn't tell them? he thought. What if they don't let me camp on my own again? But he hated not telling the truth, and he would have to tell his parents something about his two days in the bush. He could not imagine leaving out the most interesting part of his adventure. Besides, he wanted to tell them about his new friends.

Just then Matthew realised that the valley through which they were walking looked familiar. He couldn't be sure, but there was something about it that he felt he knew. No-name said something and pointed up ahead. Matthew looked up and was surprised to see his own bicycle, still leaning against the tree where he had left it.

'You've brought us right back to Goanna Gorge!' he said in surprise. 'I had no idea how close we were.'

'Really?' said No-name. Matthew walked over to his bike. It was as if he had been separated from it for months instead of just twenty-four hours. When he turned around to thank No-name, she had already gone.

Chapter 4 – Home

Matthew listened; he could hear nothing but the wind and the call of a bird. He wanted to call out to No-name, but he changed his mind. If she had gone, she must have her reasons. Even so, he stood waiting for several minutes in case she came back. Then he started to climb down again to the pool in the gorge, where he had left his belongings.

He stood near the water's edge, and was surprised at how different he now felt. It was as if the adventures of the past twenty-four hours had somehow changed him. Discovering the rock paintings, which had so excited him yesterday, now seemed much less important. His night alone in the bush was much more important. And, he suddenly realised, the last few hours with No-name and her grandmother had been just as important. For some reason, he was certain he would meet No-name again.

When Matthew looked behind the bushes where he had left his backpack and sleeping-bag, they were not there. He looked around, but he knew this was the right place. The grass was *flattened* from the weight of his things. Someone had taken them.

At weekends and holiday times people sometimes came to Goanna Gorge for a swim or a picnic. Perhaps someone else had come yesterday, after he had left. For a while he thought about all that would happen when he turned up at home without his backpack and sleeping-bag. Now there was no choice – he would have to tell his parents what had happened, to explain how he

flatten, make or become flat

had lost everything. He turned and started to climb up the gorge. Then he pushed his bike onto the road and started his long ride home. As he rode he watched the sun sink towards the hills to the west, and finally disappear behind them. Slowly the sky changed from blue to yellow, then orange, then deep red. By the time he reached his own house, it was dark.

Matthew's parents were about to sit down to the evening meal when he walked in.

'We were just going to send out a search party,' said his father happily. 'Your mother was starting to get worried. Well, did you have a good time?'

'It was fantastic,' said Matthew. 'But nothing like I imagined.'

'Were you warm enough last night?' asked his mother, smiling happily now that her son was back.

Matthew hesitated. 'Well, no, actually, I was cold.'

'Sleeping-bag no good?' asked his father, surprised. 'Where is it, anyway?'

'Dad, I've got something to tell you. And Mum. Don't get mad at me until I've told you the whole story.'

'Don't tell me you lost it? And where's your backpack?'

'Well – I think they were *stolen*.'

'Stolen? How could they be stolen? That's a couple of hundred dollars you're talking about!'

'I know, Dad, and I'm really sorry. It's a long story.'

'Well, if it's a long story you'd better tell us over dinner,' said Matthew's mother. 'Are you hungry?'

'Yes, very hungry.'

steal, (stole, stolen), take someone else's belongings without permission

'Well?' asked his father, after a few minutes' silent eating.

'You know you said you were going to send out a search party?' Matthew reminded him.

'That was just a joke because you said you'd be back by sunset, and your mother was getting worried. What of it?'

'Well, you nearly did have to send one.'

'What do you mean?'

'Matthew, you didn't get lost?' his mother asked.

'Yes, I did,' Matthew said. 'I got lost yesterday. I had to spend the night in the bush.'

'Not without your sleeping-bag?' his mother said.

'Yes, that's just it. I left my things back near Goanna Gorge pool while I went exploring. And then – I got lost and couldn't get back.'

'You told us you were going to Goanna Gorge,' his father said angrily. 'You didn't say anything about going off exploring on your own. You know what we would have said about that!'

'I know. It was silly how it happened. I went along the valley looking for those rock paintings you told me about. I found them, too.' Matthew paused. 'But then, instead of going back the same way, I tried to follow the valley along the top, and I climbed a hill and somehow lost my way. I still don't know where I went wrong.'

'This country is so dangerous,' said his mother, shaking her head. 'Thank God you're safe. Think what might have happened! You had your water-bottle with you, I hope?'

'Yes, of course.'

'Well, how did you find your way back?'

'I didn't. Someone found me.'

'Well, you were very lucky,' said his father. 'Who was it?'

'A girl. An Aboriginal girl, younger than me. She was hunting and found my tracks.'

'Hunting? On her own?' Matthew's father asked.

'Yes. She knows the bush like the back of her hand – it's amazing. She showed me how to make fire, too.' Matthew wanted to tell his parents about the best parts of his adventure, but they only seemed interested in what had gone wrong.

'And she took you back to Goanna Gorge?'

'Yes. Not straight away, though. She showed me where she was staying.'

'What do you mean, where she was staying?' asked Matthew's mother.

'They have a place there in the bush – her family does.'

'A blacks' camp!' Matthew's father said.

'Well, what's wrong with that?' said Matthew.

'What's wrong with it? Nothing, if you don't mind dirt.'

'It wasn't dirty,' said Matthew. 'It was just a camp, where they go at weekends. I met her grandmother. They live in town most of the time.'

'Where? At one of the reserves?'

'Well, yes. Only they're not called reserves any more.'

'There you are – dirt,' said Matthew's father.

'Oh, come on – you've never even been inside the communities!' said Matthew.

'No, and I wouldn't want to.'

'Well, never mind about that,' said Matthew's mother. 'At least you're safe. It was nice of that girl to help you, whoever she is. If you ever see her again, you must thank her for us. Maybe we could give her a little present.'

'If she hasn't got one already,' said Matthew's father.

'What do you mean?'

'You still haven't told us how you lost your things.'

'They were gone when I got back to Goanna Gorge. Someone must have come yesterday afternoon, after I'd left, and taken them.'

'Well, there's no use worrying about that,' said his mother. 'Losing your things is the least of it. What if you'd fallen and broken your leg, or been bitten by a snake? Or what if you'd left your water-bottle behind?'

'But I didn't!' Matthew reminded her.

'Well, I hope you've learned something, Matthew,' said his father. 'I thought you had more sense than to go off walking in the bush on your own. No compass, no sleeping-bag. You wouldn't have got hurt if you'd stayed at Goanna Gorge, where you said you were going to be.'

'I didn't get hurt!' said Matthew.

'You got lost, didn't you?'

'But I got found again.'

'That was just good luck. We'll have to think twice about letting you go off on your own again.'

'He's not going, and that's that,' said his mother.

That night Matthew lay in his warm bed and remembered how cold he had been the previous night. Yet it wasn't just the cold he remembered. He looked up at the *ceiling* and tried to imagine he could see through it

ceiling, ['siːlɪŋ] see picture, page 34

to the stars beyond. But the streetlight outside his window lit up his room, and the ceiling remained a ceiling. He remembered the walk through the bush with the strange girl, No-name. And the goanna she had tracked down and killed. He wondered what Nick and the others would say when he told them. They'd be sick with *envy*.

Matthew sat up in bed. 'I'm going to learn about the bush,' he said to himself. 'I'll ask No-name to teach me!'

envy, ['envɪ] feeling of wanting what someone else has

Chapter 5 – No-name Again

Over the next few days, Matthew often thought about No-name. Twice he cycled to Two-mile, where she had told him she lived. The community was like a small village with a fence around it. At the *entrance*, there was a sign with the community name, Piyirnwarnti, which he couldn't pronounce. For the first time, Matthew wondered why it was there. Why did most of the black people live in little communities instead of having houses in the town like everyone else? Wasn't a reserve the same thing as a ghetto? He'd heard of Jewish ghettos in Europe, and black ghettos in America, but he wasn't sure what they were like. He'd have to ask someone.

He watched for No-name in the streets. Whenever he saw a group of black girls walking together, he searched their faces for the one he knew, but hers was never among them. Doing this made him realise how little attention he had paid to the black kids, for he recognised few of them. He thought about Nick and the others. They weren't particularly friendly with the black kids. The black kids stick to themselves, too, he thought as he rode home. Maybe they don't want to mix with us. Yet No-name had been so friendly, out in the bush.

When Nick came back from his trip to Darwin with his parents, he went to Matthew's house to tell him about it.

Matthew listened while Nick described the places he had visited. 'Yeah, sounds great,' said Matthew when

entrance, opening, such as a gate, door, etc., by which people enter

Nick was done. 'I didn't go away, but I had a bit of an adventure here.'

'Really? What did you get up to?'

Matthew told Nick briefly about his trip to Goanna Gorge, and how he got lost and found again. Nick was so interested in hearing all about fire-making and hunting that he forgot to tease his friend for getting lost in the first place.

'You wouldn't think the black kids here could do all those things,' he said. 'I thought they just hung round town all the time.'

'Yeah,' said Matthew. 'No wonder some of them don't show much interest in school. Who'd want to be learning social studies when you could be out hunting!'

Four days after his adventure in the bush, Matthew got a call from the police station.

'Did you report the *theft* of a backpack and sleeping-bag last weekend?' asked the sergeant, who was a friend of Matthew's father.

'Yes,' said Matthew, though it was actually his father who had reported the theft. 'Have you found them?' He was surprised.

'We think we might have them here, if you'd like to come over and identify them.'

'I'll come straight away,' said Matthew. He jumped onto his bike at once.

At the police station the sergeant led Matthew into an interview room behind the office. On the table lay the lost belongings. But it wasn't these that caught Matthew's attention. Sitting on a chair against the wall

theft, taking someone else's belongings, stealing

by the table was No-name.

'Hello!' said Matthew, surprised. 'What are you doing here?'

'You know this girl?' asked the sergeant.

Matthew nodded. 'Yes, I know her. She found me last weekend when I was lost.'

'Did she now? Well, it seems she found more than just you.' The sergeant nodded towards the things on the table. 'Your things were at her house.'

For a moment Matthew was *puzzled*. Then he realised what the sergeant was getting at. 'She didn't take them,' he said without hesitating.

The sergeant gave him a funny look. 'What makes you so sure about that?'

puzzled, ['pʌzld] unable to understand something

'I just know,' said Matthew, unable to explain. 'That's right, isn't it?' he asked the girl. But No-name sat with her head hanging down and didn't answer.

The sergeant led Matthew back to the office and shut the door. 'You can't *trust* these people,' he told him. 'Just because they're friendly doesn't mean you can trust them. They can smile at you and steal from you at the same time, you know.'

'I don't believe it!' Matthew said. 'She wouldn't steal from me. Besides,' he suddenly remembered, 'she didn't have a chance. My things were already gone when I left her.' He described his meeting with No-name, and how she had taken him back to Goanna Gorge.

'You say she disappeared. She probably went straight down to the waterhole ahead of you, and stole your things before you even got there.'

'She couldn't have. There's only one way down, and she didn't go that way. Anyway, there wasn't time.'

'Only one way down that you know about,' said the sergeant. 'These blackfellers have their own ways of doing things.'

'But she didn't even know I'd left anything down there,' Matthew said. 'She only knew about the bike.'

'You say she saw your tracks and knew you were lost. She probably found your belongings first, and hid them in her camp before she went looking for you.'

'I tell you, she didn't steal them,' said Matthew. 'Look, can I go back and speak to her? I'm sure she'll be able to explain.'

'Well,' said the sergeant, 'we're not going to *charge*

trust, believe or have confidence in
charge, state officially that someone has broken a law

her this time, seeing as we've *recovered* everything. She's too young, and she looks a bit simple.'

'Simple?' Matthew was amazed. 'She's not simple! She's one of the cleverest girls I know!'

Again the sergeant looked at him oddly. 'You're sure it's the same girl? Frances Bulu?'

Frances, thought Matthew. So that's her real name. He wasn't going to admit he didn't know it. 'Of course that's her. Let me go and talk to her,' said Matthew.

'You can have a couple of minutes, but leave the door open.'

Matthew went back into the interview room, and the sergeant continued doing his work in the office. Matthew stood looking at the girl, but she didn't look at him.

'No-name – Frances – whatever you call yourself – just tell me what happened.' No-name sat with her head down, looking at her hands. She didn't speak. 'Why won't you talk to me? I know you didn't take my things.'

Still No-name hung her head.

'I went to the community at Two-mile looking for you.' The girl gave no sign of having heard him. 'I want to be your friend,' he said. No-name hung her head even lower.

Matthew sat in a chair near her and leaned forward. He realised with a shock that she was crying. She made no sound, but *tears* dropped slowly, one by one, onto her dress.

'Hey, I didn't mean to make you cry,' he said.

Just at that moment the sergeant put his head in at

recover, get back (something lost or stolen)
tear, [tɪə] drop of salty liquid coming from the eye

the door. 'How are you getting on?'

Matthew got up. 'She's upset,' he said. 'She won't talk to me.' He left the room.

'What I can't understand is why the police went to her house,' said Matthew at tea that evening.

'They had a good idea who she was,' said his father.

Matthew didn't understand.

'When I reported your missing things,' his father explained.

'You mean you told the police she had taken them?'

'She had, hadn't she?'

'No!' said Matthew. 'I don't believe it.'

'Well, there they are.' His father nodded towards Matthew's bedroom, where he had put his recovered belongings.

'We know how you feel,' said Matthew's mother. 'That girl helped you, and you thought you could trust her. You're *disappointed*, but that's the way these people are.'

'The fact is,' said his father, 'your friend, who found you when you were lost, also turns out to be a *thief*. That's life.'

Matthew said nothing more, but inside he was still very angry. He knew No-name hadn't stolen anything. He felt that he could trust her. He was also sure she hadn't had the chance to climb down into Goanna Gorge and take his backpack and sleeping-bag before he got there. She didn't even know where they were. And she would hardly have come looking for him in the bush

disappointed, sad at not seeing one's hopes come true
thief, [θiːf] person who steals

if she had stolen his things earlier. Besides, none of his things had been in her camp, he was sure of that. And where else would she have left them? But it was no use arguing with adults who had made up their minds.

He left the table as soon as he could and went to his room. He looked through his backpack again. Everything was still there, just as he had packed it. Nothing seemed to have been taken at all.

'Any thief would have emptied it to see what was in it,' Matthew said to himself. He thought of No-name as he had seen her at the police station. So different from the smiling young girl he had followed through the bush. She probably thinks I put the police on to her, he thought. No wonder she wouldn't speak to me. She'll never want to speak to me again.

Matthew made up his mind to find No-name the next morning and to talk to her. He couldn't bear to leave so many misunderstandings between them.

Chapter 6 – A Mystery *Solved*

The following morning, Matthew was up at the Two-mile community again at seven. While he was making up his mind whether to go in, two young men in jeans and cowboy hats came towards the gate. They looked at Matthew, and one of them nodded.

'Excuse me,' Matthew said, and they both stopped. 'I'm looking for a girl called ...' He thought for a moment. What had the policeman called her? Frances something. 'Er, I think her name is Frances.' Then he

solve, find a solution to or explanation for

wanted to bite his tongue. She had told him people didn't use her name since someone had died. But he couldn't remember how to pronounce the other name she had told him.

'That young Kumunyjayi?' said one of the men.

'Yes, that's her!' Matthew nodded. 'Do you know her?'

'She's my sister,' said the other man.

'Really?' said Matthew.

'Yeah. You want to talk to her?'

Matthew nodded again.

'She's in that blue house over there.'

'Well, thanks.' Matthew nervously pushed his bike in through the gate and towards the house No-name's brother had pointed out. He felt sure everyone in the community was looking at him. He half expected someone to tell him to go away, but no one did.

As Matthew approached the blue house, he saw that the door was wide open and there were several people in the backyard. No-name wasn't among them, but Matthew was happy to recognise her grandmother. The old woman saw him coming and called out to him. She seemed just as friendly as she had been the day he had met her in the bush. At least the whole family didn't hate him.

'You looking for that Napangarti?' she asked. 'She's not here.'

Matthew had no idea what Napangarti meant, but he knew the old woman must be talking about her granddaughter. 'Oh dear.' He wondered why her brother hadn't told him that. 'Do you know where she is?'

The old woman shook her head, but said nothing. Matthew wanted to ask more questions, but he didn't like to do so in case she thought him *rude*. Instead he said goodbye to her and pushed his bike out through the entrance.

The following Monday, school started again. Matthew went off on his bicycle feeling that the holiday, which had started off so well, had turned out to be a disappointment. But he met Nick at the school gate, and before long the two boys were in a circle of classmates exchanging news. Matthew's adventure seemed even more exciting the way Nick retold it.

'And then this black girl appeared out of nowhere and carried him off to her camp in the bush!'

During the morning *recess*, his friends left to play basketball. Matthew was sitting by himself eating an apple when he saw someone come towards him.

'No-name!' he said out loud. 'What are you doing here?'

No-name sat down next to him and smiled just as she had done the first time he met her. There was no sign in her face that she was angry. It was as if she had completely forgotten what had happened at the police station. Matthew could not get it out of his mind.

'How are you?' he asked. 'And how come you're here at school?' No-name laughed, and Matthew suddenly realised that she was a pupil. Of course, she must be! It hadn't occurred to him that No-name, the girl who had seemed so at home in the bush, also went to school. She must be in a class a year or two below his. Yet Matthew had never noticed her before. She had been just one of the black kids running around the yard.

rude, not polite, not showing respect, with bad manners
recess, ['ri:ses] short break between classes in school

No-name still hadn't said anything.

'What happened at the police station?' Matthew asked her.

The girl's face went serious for a moment, then she shrugged. 'They let me go home.' She smiled again.

'I'm sorry about all that,' Matthew said, wanting to give her an explanation. But No-name didn't seem to expect one. 'I came looking for you the other day,' he told her.

No-name nodded. 'Grandmother told me.'

'I met your brother,' he went on. 'He told me you were at home.'

No-name smiled. 'Who was that?'

Matthew was puzzled. She must know her own brother. 'Tall fellow, *curly* hair ...'

'He had boots?'

Matthew thought for a moment. 'Yes, cowboy boots.'

No-name smiled again. 'That's Alfie. But he's not really my brother,' she said. 'I call him brother. But he's my *cousin*-brother.'

'Your cousin-brother?'

'Mm. His mother's sister is my mother.' She thought a moment, then went on. 'But not really sister. They call one another sister.'

'I see,' said Matthew, not at all sure what she meant. He felt that here was a different way of seeing the world.

'That brother found your things,' said No-name suddenly.

Matthew looked at her. At last he was going to learn

curly, (of hair) having curls, having a curved shape
cousin, ['kʌzən] child of the brother/sister of one's mother/father

the truth. 'Your brother?' he repeated. 'Alfie? The one with the boots?'

No-name nodded. 'That day, when I found you. My brother was hunting near the waterhole, and he picked up your things. He didn't know they were yours. He was thinking someone had left them behind. But I told him afterwards – those are Matthew's things! He was sorry then. But it was too late – you were already gone.'

'He brought my things to your camp?' said Matthew.

No-name nodded. 'Mm.'

'Why did he do that?' He was still uncertain. No-name shrugged and looked away.

Now Matthew understood. No-name's brother had taken his things, perhaps thinking they'd been lost, perhaps just because he liked the look of them.

'So you took them home?' he said.

'Yeah, to keep them for you. I couldn't leave them in the bush. Someone might steal them.'

'The police thought you did.'

'I know. I was home by myself. The police came to my grandmother's house. They asked me for your things, and I showed them. Then they took me to the police station.'

'Why didn't you tell them it wasn't you that took them?'

'I was frightened. They might have *blamed* my brother for stealing. They might have locked him up. I never said anything.'

'You don't know where I live, do you?' asked Matthew.

'Yeah, I know. But I can't go to your house.' No-name laughed.

blame, consider (someone) responsible (for something bad)

'Why not?'

She shrugged. 'Your father might get wild with us.'

Matthew said nothing. He couldn't imagine his father getting wild exactly, but he suddenly saw him from the girl's point of view. How frightening a prison officer must seem to her. He remembered how afraid he had been of going inside the community where No-name lived. A simple thing like knocking on his front door would be just as frightening for No-name. Probably worse. And then having to explain how she happened to have Matthew's missing things. No, he could see she couldn't have done that.

Chapter 7 – Jampijin

Matthew told his father what had really happened to his belongings. 'She was keeping my things for me.'

'I suppose you believe that story,' his father said.

'Of course I do,' said Matthew angrily. 'I know it's true.'

'And I suppose you believe you'd have got everything back if the police hadn't found it for you?'

'Yes,' said Matthew. 'She was waiting until she saw me.'

'It would have been a long wait, I can tell you.' Matthew's father went back to reading his paper.

'She'd have seen me at school.'

'Two weeks later?'

His father would not accept that No-name and her family were too *shy* or too frightened to come to the

shy, nervous or uncomfortable when together with others

house. 'Why should they be shy?' he asked. 'They know you. They know where you live. They had to drive right past this house on their way back to Two-mile. Of course they weren't going to give anything back. You're too trusting, my boy. You'll learn the hard way.'

Matthew *held his tongue* with difficulty. There was no arguing with his father. He went to his room.

After that meeting in the schoolyard, Matthew often saw No-name. She didn't seem to go to school every day. Even when he saw her there, she didn't always come and speak to him, and never when he was with any of his friends. She seemed shyer and less sure of herself than she had been in the bush. The memory of the day they had met was never far from Matthew's thoughts. He wanted to go into the bush again. He knew, too, that he only wanted to go with No-name.

One day after school he walked with No-name, pushing his bike, as far as the reserve. He hesitated at the entrance, but No-name seemed to expect him to go in with her, so he pushed his bike beside her up to the blue house. A few people waved or nodded at him. He felt pleased to be recognised.

'Ah, Jampijin!' came the voice of No-name's grandmother as they approached the house.

'What's that your grandmother calls me?' asked Matthew. 'It sounds like Jamby something.'

No-name laughed as she had done that first time. 'Jampijin,' she said. 'That's a skin name.'

'A skin name?' said Matthew, puzzled. 'What's that?'

hold one's tongue, keep quiet, say nothing

'Everybody's got a skin name,' said No-name.

'Yes? What's yours?'

'Me, I'm Napangarti.' No-name laughed again. Matthew remembered her grandmother had used a term like that when he had visited the reserve before.

'What does it mean, to be Jampijin?' he asked her.

She hesitated.

'Jampijin, he's right for Napangarti!' said her grandmother, who had been following the conversation. No-name laughed again.

'Right? Right for what?'

'Jampijin and Napangarti, they're husband and wife,' explained the old woman. 'Napangarti marries Jampijin!' She laughed while Matthew and No-name tried to hide their embarrassment.

The following day, during library period, Matthew looked for books on Australian Aboriginal culture. He wasn't sure where to start looking, so when the *librarian* came past he asked her where he could find out something about 'skin' names. She seemed to know what he was talking about, and soon pulled down a book on Kimberley history.

'I think this one has a good chapter on the Aboriginal people before white people came here,' she said. Together they found a section called *Kinship* Systems.

'This must be it,' said Matthew. 'Thanks.'

The book described the different kinds of relationships recognised in Aboriginal societies. Now Matthew understood what No-name had meant when she'd said her brother was 'not really her brother' but her 'cousin-brother'. It turned out that one's father's brother was

librarian, [laɪˈbreərɪən] person in charge of a library
kinship, family relationship

also called 'father', and one's mother's sister was called 'mother'. It followed that one called the children of these 'fathers' or 'mothers' brother and sister instead of cousin.

Matthew read how everyone in the whole society was classified in relationship to everyone else. These relationships were determined by the 'skin' or section/subsection system. The chapter went on to explain about the different skin groups '... still in use among people, mainly in the north of the country, where traditions are more *intact* than in places where Europeans have lived for much longer ... A person belonging to one section should only marry a person from the opposite one.' He saw that each skin name was written opposite that of its marriage group. He searched until he found Jampijin. Opposite Jampijin was the name Napangarti – No-name's skin. Matthew learned that being Jampijin made him a possible husband not only to No-name but to most other Napangartis.

'Jampijin,' he said to himself *proudly*. 'Jampijin.' He liked the sound of it. He had a skin name that related him to everyone in No-name's community. That was something he wasn't going to tell his father.

One morning when he saw No-name with a couple of other girls outside the schoolyard, Matthew stopped to speak with her. The other girls left.

'When are you going out into the bush again?' he asked.

intact, whole, untouched, unchanged
proudly, with a high opinion of oneself

'We go every weekend, nearly,' she told him.

'Every weekend?' Matthew hesitated. 'I might ride down to Goanna Gorge again on Saturday,' he said. 'Maybe I'll find you there?'

'You might get lost,' said No-name. 'What about you coming with us this weekend?'

Matthew's heart jumped. To go camping out with No-name and her family was something he had not *dared* think of. 'You think I can? What about your parents?'

'Of course you can come. I'll tell Mummy.'

When Matthew asked his parents if he could spend a weekend with No-name's family, they were amazed.

'But they stole your things!' said his mother.

'They didn't steal them,' said Matthew. 'Someone in her family picked them up. That wasn't her *fault*. I've explained all that to you before.'

'What's wrong with Nick and your other friends?' asked his father. 'Why can't you go camping with them?'

'Nothing's wrong with Nick. But he hasn't asked me to go camping, Frances has. What's wrong with her?'

'We haven't met her, or her family.'

Matthew hesitated. He didn't really want his parents to meet No-name's family. He felt sure they wouldn't know what to say to them. But if that was the only way they'd let him go ...

'You could meet them on Friday,' he said. 'Anyway, I know them. They helped me when I was lost, don't forget.'

dare, be brave (i.e. not afraid) enough to (do something)
fault, [fɔːlt] responsibility for something bad happening

'Hm,' said his father. 'That's true enough. You're probably safer with them than walking around in the bush on your own.'

'Of course I am!' Matthew said.

'What will you get to eat?' his mother asked. 'Snakes and lizards?'

'I hope so,' said Matthew, who wanted to learn about living in the bush. 'But I'll take some other food as well.'

'Don't expect to have anything left,' his father said.

Matthew couldn't see any point in taking food away for the weekend and then bringing some of it back again. But neither of his parents had said he couldn't go, so he said nothing.

After school on Friday, Matthew hurried home and was all ready waiting with his backpack and sleeping-bag when four o'clock came. No-name had told him that was about the time they'd drive past his house. He had promised to wait outside so that she wouldn't have to knock at the door. His father would still be at work until six, and Matthew asked his mother not to make a *fuss* when the car came. 'Just say hello or something,' he said. 'Don't ask them a whole lot of questions. They might think you don't trust them.'

But four o'clock, then five o'clock came and went, and there was no sign of the old truck. Matthew walked to the end of the road and back. He hardly dared to go into the house in case the truck came when he was not there and drove off without him. But at last darkness fell and he gave up and went inside.

fuss, unnecessary excitement

'I told you you can't trust them,' said his father when he came home.

'Something must have happened,' said Matthew, standing by the window and watching the road.

'Never mind,' said his mother. She seemed glad he wasn't going after all. 'You can go for a ride somewhere tomorrow on your own, or with one of your real friends.'

'Frances is my real friend,' said Matthew. He didn't call her No-name to his parents. That was something special he kept to himself.

Chapter 8 – Back to the Bush

The following morning, just as Matthew was pushing his bicycle onto the road, a car pulled up in front of the house. It was the old truck loaded with people, *jerry cans* of *petrol* and piles of bags. No-name was seated on top of the bags on the back. She waved, smiling. Matthew leaned his bike against the fence and went up to her. Everyone was smiling at him.

'You coming?' asked the girl, as if this was the arrangement they had made.

'Of course!' Matthew didn't hesitate. While the truck waited outside, he ran indoors to get his things.

'They're here!' he told his mother. 'I'll see you tomorrow.' Before she could say anything, Matthew ran into the kitchen for some food and put it in his bag. He ran outside, looking back to see the worried face of his

jerry can, (in Australia) special container for petrol or water
petrol, liquid used to power a car

mother, who was standing at the door. He gave her a quick wave and ran to the truck.

No-name took his backpack and sleeping-bag and put them in the back of the truck. Her grandmother smiled and nodded at him. There were two other women in the back, and several children of different ages.

'This is my mother.' Matthew shook hands with the woman whose face looked like No-name's. 'And this is my *aunt*. And this is another aunt.' When he had shaken hands with all the women, Matthew got in in front, where a space had been made for him in the passenger seat. He sat down next to a tall young man. Matthew recognised the boots at once. No-name's cousin-brother Alfie! He looked up at his face, and was surprised to see the young man smiling at him. Alfie held out his hand, and Matthew took it. Not a word had been said, but he knew they understood one another, and were now friends.

Between the young man and the driver was a boy a year or two younger than Matthew. He looked at Matthew curiously and smiled, but said nothing.

The driver, a big man wearing a dark brown cowboy hat, leaned across and shook hands with Matthew. 'G'day, young fellow,' he said, giving him a warm smile. Matthew supposed he must be No-name's father.

As they drove, Matthew looked out at the countryside around them. Just after crossing the *creek* north of Goanna Gorge, the truck slowed down and turned off along a bush track Matthew had never noticed before. Some way along the track, the truck pulled up. No-name's two aunts got out, with Alfie, some of the chil-

aunt, [ɑːnt] sister of one's father or mother
creek, small river

dren and a pile of bags. They seemed to be camping independently. After helping with the unloading, the older man got back into the driver's seat and they drove on. After a while they came to the camp No-name had brought Matthew to the day she had found him. Everyone got down from the truck and unloaded the bags. Then the man started working on the truck's engine.

'That your father?' Matthew asked No-name.

No-name laughed and shook her head. 'He's my uncle. My mother's brother.' She nodded towards the boy Matthew had sat next to in the truck. 'Peter, that's his son.'

'Haven't you got a father?' Matthew asked.

'Yeah, I've got a father.' No-name paused, then added, 'But he's in prison.' She smiled.

For a moment, Matthew said nothing. No-name's father in prison, in the same place where his own father worked? He felt his face burning.

'I didn't know. My father never said anything.'

'Maybe he doesn't know.'

'He must know. He knows all the prisoners. What's your father's name? Isn't it the same as yours?'

'No. My father's got another name. I got my name from my mother.'

'Bulu, isn't it?'

No-name nodded. 'But my father's name is Freddy Ajax. He comes from Warntu. That's his country.'

'Warntu?' said Matthew. 'That's right down in the desert, isn't it?'

'Yes. He's a desert man, my father. He was born in the desert.'

'What about your mother? Is she a desert woman, too?'

No-name shook her head. 'No, she comes from round here. But she worked on a *station* once. Same station as my father. That's how my father met her.'

'I see.' Matthew thought a bit. 'How long is he doing in prison?'

'He will get out before Christmas, maybe. They gave him twelve months this time.'

'This time? You mean he's been in prison before?'

'Yeah, plenty of times. The *grog* gets him into trouble. Only for one week, two weeks, something like that. But this time they gave him twelve months.'

Matthew wondered what he had done, but he didn't ask. He was afraid it might be something No-name wouldn't want to tell him. He always seemed to be asking questions, and he had noticed that No-name never asked him questions about his family. Perhaps it was bad manners to ask as many questions as he did.

No-name's uncle said a few words to her mother and got into the driver's seat again. Peter, No-name and Matthew got in the back. The truck started and was soon driving along the track past the camp. Suddenly, No-name gave a cry and the truck stopped. A *rifle* appeared at the driver's window, and Matthew looked in the direction in which it pointed. At once he saw what had caught No-name's attention: under a tree stood a large *bush turkey*. There was a shot and the turkey fell down. No-name's uncle walked over to it and lifted it up by the neck. Then he threw it over his shoulder and carried it back to the truck.

station, (in Australia or New Zealand) large cattle or sheep farm
grog, (in Australia) strong alcoholic drink
rifle, ['raɪfl] gun with a long barrel (see picture, page 56)
bush turkey, large black Australian bird with a red head and yellow neck, that looks like a turkey (see picture, page 56)

No-name's mother was very happy when she saw the turkey. 'Warawu!' she said, in a tone that made it sound like Hurrah!

'You want to help clean it?' No-name asked, pointing at the turkey, which Peter was holding. Matthew followed her. He had never *plucked* a bird before, and found it harder than it looked. When the turkey was naked and white, Peter carried it to the fire. His father picked it up by the neck and held it over the fire. Then he covered it with charcoal and hot sand. Matthew went to his backpack and pulled out the fresh food he had brought.

pluck, pull the feathers off (a bird)

No-name's grandmother had disappeared while the truck was away from the camp. Now she came back, carrying a plastic bag filled with nuts of some sort. She emptied the bag on the ground.

'You know tartaku?' the old woman asked Matthew, who picked one up, examined it and shook his head.

'They call it bush coconut,' said No-name. 'You want to try one?'

The old woman sent Peter to the truck for a hammer and then used it to break open one of the nuts. Inside was something soft and pink. The old woman passed the opened nut to Matthew.

'Eat it!' No-name told him. Matthew hesitated, so she picked up a second opened nut and put the contents in her mouth. 'Good one!' she said, smiling. Matthew shook out the pink contents into his mouth and *swallowed* it. Not *delicious*, but not bad.

It was only when the old woman opened another nut in which there were little insects with wings that Matthew realised what they actually were. The pink things he had just eaten must have been the *larvae* of those insects. No-name offered another nut to Matthew, who shook his head, then swallowed it herself.

No one had yet explained to Matthew why they had not come out to the bush the night before as planned, and he asked No-name now. She shrugged. 'No money,' she said. 'We had no money for petrol.'

larva

swallow, cause (food or drink) to go from the mouth down the throat
delicious, [dɪˈlɪʃəs] with a good taste or smell

Matthew was shocked. No money! He had never in his life heard his own parents say they had no money. It was true, they often told him they couldn't afford to buy a particular thing. But it was usually something big – a washing machine or a new car. Never had they been unable to go anywhere because they couldn't afford petrol. He couldn't imagine how it would feel to have no money at all, even for one day. He wondered how No-name's family had managed to get money for petrol on a Saturday morning.

'The boss gave us two jerry cans,' explained No-name.

'Boss?'

'Yeah – community boss – chairman. He gave us some. My uncle can pay him next time.'

'Have you always lived at the reserve?' asked Matthew.

'No, not always. When I was a little girl, we lived in the bush. My father and my mother worked on a station, like I said.'

'What did they do?'

'My father was doing any kind of work: riding horses, making fences ... and my mother was working in the house. Washing plates, cleaning, all that.'

'Why did you leave the station?'

No-name shrugged. 'My father fell off a horse and hurt his back. He was in hospital for three months. He couldn't work any more. No more riding horses, the doctor told him. They wouldn't let us stay after that. We had to go and live in town.'

'Your father never had a job since then?'

'No. We get *Social Security*.'

Matthew wanted to ask more, but he didn't want to

be rude. No one had asked him any questions about himself. They all just seemed to take him as he was.

When the turkey was done, Peter pulled some leafy branches from a tree and arranged them on the ground. No-name pulled the turkey out from under the sand and laid it on the leaves. Her uncle cut up the turkey and handed the lower part of one of the legs to Matthew. Matthew took a bite from the leg. The meat was strong-tasting and more like *beef* than chicken.

After the meal, everyone was so full that there was only one sensible thing to do, and that was to rest. One by one people found themselves a spot under a tree and lay down on the ground. No-name lay next to her grandmother, and Matthew found a place under the same tree as Peter. He looked up through the leaves at the blue sky. There was nothing he wanted more at this moment. Smiling to himself with quiet happiness, he soon fell asleep.

Chapter 9 – *Emu* in the Sky

Matthew woke to the sounds of other people moving about the camp, and for a moment he was unsure of where he was. Then it all fell into place like a *jigsaw puzzle* putting itself together. He sat up and looked around. The sun was low in the western sky, and every-

Social Security, government money paid to people who are unemployed, old, etc.
beef, meat of farm cattle
emu, ['iːmjuː] very large Australian bird that cannot fly (see picture, page 60)
jigsaw puzzle, ['dʒɪgsɔː ˌpʌzl] picture cut into many pieces to be fitted together

emu

one else had either gone or was going away from the camp into the surrounding bush. Matthew hurried after No-name. She was carrying a wooden hunting stick, and she was looking at the ground. Matthew wondered what she saw.

'Where are we going?' he asked.

'I'll show you something,' was all she would say.

Before long No-name stopped and made a sign for Matthew to keep quiet. Then she walked very slowly, apparently heading for a tree several metres away. Matthew, following at a distance, saw a big hole dug into the ground at the base of the tree. No-name got down on her knees and looked inside the hole. She put in her hand, got hold of something and pulled it out. Then she handed Matthew a little *puppy*.

'A little *dingo*!' said Matthew. 'It's beautiful. But how did you know it was here?'

'My uncle told me. He had seen the hole before, when the puppies were just born. He couldn't go near them then. The mother dingo will bite you!'

'Where's the mother now?' Matthew looked around.

puppy, young dog
dingo, Australian wild dog

'She's gone hunting.'

No-name felt around in the hole again, and pulled out a second puppy like the first.

Then Matthew had a terrible thought. 'You're not going to kill them, are you?'

No-name laughed and shook her head. 'People used to eat dingos, before. But today we don't kill them. Poor fellows. We let them walk round. Some people eat them all right, but not us.'

'That's good. I wouldn't like to eat this little fellow.'

They put the puppies down and watched them disappear into their hole.

They spent the rest of the afternoon walking slowly back, looking for tracks, but nothing caught No-name's interest. The other members of the family returned one by one. The sun went down and stars appeared. After eating the leftover meat and drinking the last tea, everyone got ready for sleep. No-name lay near her mother and grandmother at one side of the fire.

Matthew lay down not far from Peter and his father. Unused to going to bed so early – he thought it could be no later than eight o'clock – he lay awake for a long time. He watched the sky, and picked out different *constellations* that he knew. He thought of all the generations of human beings that had lain on the ground at night and looked at the stars, as he did now. The artists of Goanna Gorge had done the same.

Then he heard No-name's voice. 'Matthew?'

'Yes,' said Matthew, going towards the voice. 'I can't sleep.'

No-name's hand touched his arm. 'Yeah.' Matthew sat down beside her, and for a while they didn't speak.

'Look at all those stars,' he said at last.

'You know the emu?' asked No-name.

'Emu?' said Matthew, not sure what she meant.

'The big emu in the sky?'

'No, where?'

'See that dark place, near the Cross?'

'Near the *Southern Cross*? Yes.'

'Well, that's its head,' said No-name.

'The emu's head?' said Matthew, not seeing. 'Where's its body?'

constellation, group of stars, often with a name (e.g. the Great Bear)
Southern Cross, name of a constellation in the southern hemisphere in the shape of a cross

'Right along there.' No-name waved her hand across what seemed like half the sky. Matthew searched the sky. He thought at first that he was supposed to be looking for stars in a constellation shaped like an emu, and couldn't see them. No-name showed him again. 'It's all dark,' she said.

Matthew looked again, starting at the Southern Cross. Suddenly, there it was – a huge, black emu spread right across the sky. 'I can see it!' he said. 'I can see it! A giant emu!'

Just then, someone moved in the darkness and spoke. No-name answered, and then there was silence again.

'See you in the morning,' Matthew said to No-name before they separated. For a long time he lay in his sleeping-bag looking at the shape of the giant emu that had until this night been hidden from him.

The next morning, after breakfast, everyone packed up the truck again. Matthew was surprised they were leaving so early.

'We're going hunting halfway,' No-name explained. This time Matthew climbed onto the back with No-name and Peter, and the two women sat in the front seat.

The truck drove through the bush, back along the way they had come the previous day. As they came to a turn they stopped. A few moments later, the people who had got off there yesterday reappeared from the bush, carrying all their belongings.

'They got their own camp in there,' No-name explained to Matthew.

They headed north for a few kilometres. At Omega

Creek they turned off west again, down a rough track along the creek. When they stopped and everyone got out, Matthew followed No-name, who carried her wooden hunting stick. She stopped every now and then to point out to him something new.

'Snake!' she said suddenly, looking at the ground near some grass. Matthew looked, too. All he could see was that the sand had been slightly flattened in one spot. No-name was already following the track while he stood there. He ran to catch up. 'How do you know which way it's going?' he asked, but she just laughed.

'You can see which way,' she said.

Matthew was puzzled. Then he saw the track clearly: a heavy, almost straight track flattening the sand, going slightly downhill.

'See – it's going that way,' said No-name. Further on, the track went up a small hill, and here it was no longer straight, but zig-zagged from side to side. Matthew stopped and looked at it carefully. Of course, he thought. Going downhill the snake would be helped by *gravity*. Going uphill would be harder for the snake, and the tracks it made would be different. He felt pleased with himself. He was beginning to understand the sort of signs No-name must be reading all the time.

The tracks led to a hole in the ground near a bush. Breaking off a long dry stick from the bush, No-name started *poking* it into the hole carefully. 'It's here,' she said.

Matthew, who was watching the hole, saw something dark come up. 'Here it is!' he shouted excitedly.

gravity, natural force that attracts objects to the centre of the earth
poke, push (something pointed)

'It's coming out!'

No-name moved her stick again, and a *shiny* black head appeared. Matthew jumped back. The snake moved quickly out of the hole and through the grass.

'Give me that stick,' No-name said, dropping the dry one she had used. She held out her hand while keeping her eyes fixed on the snake. Matthew looked around, and saw the hunting stick lying in the grass. He quickly handed it to No-name. She held the stick for a moment, and then brought it down on the snake, just behind its head. Then she stepped on the snake's head, holding it down with her foot. She bent down, carefully took hold of the snake by its neck, then took her foot away and straightened up. She held it out for Matthew to look at. 'Black-head,' she told him.

'A black-headed python?' Matthew had seen pictures of them in books and knew they were not dangerous, but this was the first one he had seen alive. He reached out and touched it, feeling its strong body moving under his hand. He took the snake from No-name's hand, holding it just behind its head, as she had done. He looked into its black, shiny eyes, and wondered what it was feeling.

'Kill it now,' No-name told him, but Matthew shook his head.

'Can't we let it go?' he said, sounding a bit silly even to himself. He knew what the answer would be.

'It's good to eat,' No-name said and took the snake from him. Then, taking the tail in one hand, she raised the snake in the air and beat its head against the ground. She did this twice more, then threw it down.

shiny, ['ʃaɪnɪ] giving off light as if it were polished

Matthew told himself, if this was hunting, he'd have to get used to it.

No-name handed Matthew the dead snake. He hung it around his neck to carry it back to the truck.

The others were already waiting, but apart from No-name only her uncle had caught anything. He had killed two goannas he told them. No-name described killing the snake. When she came to the part about Matthew wanting to let it go, everyone laughed.

'Good meat, that one!' said her mother.

When the snake had been cooked together with a goanna, Matthew had the opportunity to taste it for himself. His stomach did not like the idea, but he forced himself to swallow a little piece. He had to admit it didn't taste bad. Even so, he felt happier eating the piece of goanna tail he was offered next.

After a rest, it was time to go home. The truck dropped off Matthew at his house, and he stood watching its lights disappear down the road before he went inside.

'How's the great white hunter?' asked his father.

'Good,' said Matthew. 'I had a great time!'

'What did you get to eat?'

'Snake, goanna, turkey ...'

'Turkey?' said his mother, surprised.

'Not supermarket turkey – bush turkey. Frances's uncle shot one.'

'I'd be *fined* if I did that,' said his father. 'They're supposed to be a *protected species*.'

'Well, you have to realise that Aboriginal people

fine, make (someone) pay money for breaking a law
protected species, [prə'tektɪd 'spiːʃiːz] animal protected by special laws

have always been hunters,' said his mother.

'Not with rifles.'

Matthew changed the subject. 'They cook everything with charcoal in the ground, then put it on a pile of leaves. No plates, no washing up.'

'That would suit you,' his mother laughed. 'I might even get used to it myself.'

'So I can go again?' Matthew looked from his mother to his father.

'I guessed that was coming,' said his father.

'We've talked about it,' said his mother. 'In one way we're not happy about the idea. But, well, you obviously enjoy it, and you seem to be learning a lot.'

'And in another way, I envy you the opportunity.' Matthew was surprised to hear his father admitting it. 'Just don't get too friendly with those people, that's all.'

'What do you mean?'

'Well, it's all very well to go out with people and learn about their way of life – living in the bush and that sort of thing – but don't start thinking you're one of them. You've got your own culture, and you'd better not forget it.'

'How could I forget it?' asked Matthew, who had been making secret plans to give up school and go off to live in the bush instead.

'We don't want you turning into a blackfeller,' said his mother. 'We're not racist or anything, but, well, people are usually much better off if they stick with their own kind.'

After that weekend, Matthew often went hunting with No-name's family. Sometimes it was just for the day, with a quick visit to their bush camp, and home by dark. Other times they camped out again overnight. Occasionally, No-name said they'd take him hunting, and then they failed to turn up. There was never any explanation unless Matthew asked for one. Usually it was that they had had no money, or the truck had broken down and needed repairs.

'You can bring your little Aboriginal friend home to tea one day, if you like,' his mother said once. 'You are always going places with her. Don't you think you should ask her back for a change?'

Matthew knew she was trying to be kind, and to make him happy. But even the way she said 'little Aboriginal friend' embarrassed him. He could just hear her saying something like that to No-name. And he could imagine how his father would behave.

'There's no way I'd bring her back here with Dad the way he is,' he told his mother. 'Her family are so friendly and easygoing. I'd die of shame if anyone made her feel uncomfortable.' He meant his mother, too, but didn't say so.

'Your father's not a bad man,' she reminded Matthew. 'He's just a bit conservative.'

'I know,' said Matthew. He knew they'd never make such a fuss about letting him spend time with Nick and his family.

Chapter 10 – Surprise Meeting

One morning Matthew got up early, worrying about an assignment he had to finish for that day. Suddenly he remembered his bicycle had a *puncture*. His father, who started work at six, was having breakfast.

'Dad, can you drop me off at school this morning on your way to work?' Matthew asked.

'You'll have to make it quick,' said his father. 'I'll be leaving in five minutes. If you're not ready you'll have to walk.'

Matthew swallowed some breakfast and picked up his schoolbag. He heard the sound of the car starting up and ran outside.

'I forgot to fill up last night!' said his father, looking at the *fuel gauge*. He backed into the road and started in the direction of the prison. He kept looking at the gauge. Matthew saw that the needle was right on empty.

'I'll drop you off and then get petrol,' his father told him. But almost before he finished speaking, the engine died and the car came to a stop. Matthew said nothing, but watched his father out of the corner of his eye. There were several seconds of silence, then Matthew's father got out of the car and stood looking at it. Matthew joined him.

'I'll take the jerry can,' Matthew offered, knowing his father always carried one in the car.

'It's a couple of miles to the roadhouse.'

'I might be able to get a lift. Anyway, Mr Franklyn will get someone to bring me back.'

puncture, ['pʌŋktʃə] small hole in a tyre made by something sharp
fuel gauge, ['fjuːəl ˌgeɪdʒ] instrument for measuring amount of petrol in a car

Matthew's father took out the jerry can and handed it to him. Matthew started off on foot. It was too early for most other people to be heading into town, but he would be unlucky if no one came along.

He heard a car approaching from the opposite direction. '*Murphy's law*,' he said to himself. The car slowed down as it came near, and he heard someone call his name. He looked up and saw several young Aboriginal men in the old car. Then he saw that the man with the hat next to the driver was No-name's cousin-brother, Alfie. He smiled at Matthew.

'Where are you going?' Alfie asked.

'To the roadhouse. We ran out of petrol.' Matthew pointed to the jerry can he was carrying.

'Where's your car?'

'Back down that way.'

'You want petrol?'

Matthew nodded. One of the young men in the back opened the door, and they all made room for Matthew. Then the car set off again, but instead of turning around to go to the petrol station, they went on in the same direction. When his father's car came into sight, they slowed down. Matthew's father was leaning against his car. As the other car pulled to a stop and he saw his son hanging out of the back window, he straightened up, surprised.

Everyone got out of the car, talking and laughing. Matthew introduced his father to Alfie, and the two men shook hands. A jerry can was brought out of the old car, and one of the young men started *syphoning*

Murphy's law, (as a joke) statement that things will go wrong if they can possibly do so

petrol from their car into the jerry can. When the can was about half full, he emptied it into the petrol tank of Matthew's father's car. Matthew's father looked embarrassed to be receiving help. When they were done, he turned around and took out his *wallet*.

syphon

'I must give you something for the petrol,' he said.

Alfie shrugged, smiling. 'No, it's all right,' he said.

But Matthew's father pushed a note into his hand. 'No, take it,' he said. 'You can't give me your petrol for nothing. You'll need to refill soon.' Alfie put the money into his pocket, and nodded his thanks.

'Well, thank you very much for your help,' Matthew's father said to the group of men.

'Yeah, thanks a lot!' said Matthew. The men got back into the old car. They waited until Matthew's father had successfully started his own engine before driving off. With smiles and waves they disappeared down the road.

Matthew's father did not speak as they continued the drive to the school. But at the gate, as Matthew climbed out with his schoolbag, his father said, 'Not a bad bunch of fellows, those friends of yours.'

syphon, ['saɪfən] draw off (a liquid) by means of a bent tube
wallet, small, flat pocket-case for keeping money in

Chapter 11 – A Shock

The weather had been getting hotter for weeks, and the end of the school year was approaching. One day when Matthew got home, he found his father home before him. He could tell that something important was being discussed.

'Your father has something to tell you,' said his mother. Matthew waited.

'We're moving,' his father told him.

Matthew didn't understand. 'Moving?' he said. 'Where to?'

'To Perth,' said his mother. 'Your father got his transfer.'

Matthew had known that his father had applied for a *promotion* and a transfer south, but he had put it out of his mind as something unlikely to happen.

'Can't be!' he said, not believing it. 'We can't go back to live in Perth!'

'What's wrong with Perth?' said his father. 'You didn't want to leave Perth when we came up here.'

'That's different. I didn't know what it was like here then. I know what Perth is like. I hate it!' he said, suddenly very angry.

'Oh, come on, Matthew, it's not that bad. You were happy there,' his mother reminded him. 'Your dad's got a promotion. Don't *spoil* it for him.'

'Yeah – congratulations, Dad.' Matthew's voice was lifeless. 'It's good for you, I know that. But can't they give you a promotion and leave you here?'

promotion, higher rank or position
spoil, ruin, make less valuable

'If you want to get on in this job you just have to be prepared to go where the promotions are.'

'Yeah, I suppose. How soon do you have to go?'

Matthew's parents looked at each other. 'Quite soon,' said his mother, not looking at him.

'How soon?'

'Matthew, we are leaving at the end of next week,' his father told him.

'Next week?' Matthew almost shouted, shocked. 'How can it be next week?'

'They need me to start as soon as possible. I know it's a bit sudden, but that's the way it is. We'd have to go sooner or later. It's nearly the end of the school year for you anyway. It doesn't make much difference.'

'What do you mean, it doesn't make much difference?' Matthew was almost in tears. 'Of course it makes a difference! It's all right for you. But I don't want to go. I just don't want to go!'

'Well, that's just too bad,' said Matthew's father. 'We're going, and that's that. You might as well get used to the idea.'

'Why do I have to go?' Matthew turned to his mother. 'Can't I stay here?'

His mother laughed. 'Of course you can't stay here on your own,' she said. 'Where would you live?'

'With Frances's family!' said Matthew suddenly, without thinking, then he wished he had kept his mouth shut.

'Don't tell me you want to stay here just so you can turn into a blackfeller!' his father said angrily.

'What's wrong with blackfellers?' Matthew shouted. 'I'd rather stay with blackfellers in the bush than be stuck in a house in Perth with a front *lawn* you have to *mow* on Sundays like everyone else!'

'You'd rather hang round with a bunch of criminals, would you?'

'What do you mean by that?' Matthew asked.

'That little thief you run around with. She's just like her father.'

Matthew could think of nothing to say. So his father had known all along.

'Freddy Ajax is the biggest *drunk* in the district. If I'd known he was her father I'd never have let you have anything to do with her in the first place.'

lawn, area of grass, usually in a garden or park
mow, [məʊ] cut (grass), usually with a machine
drunk, person who often drinks too much alcohol

'How did you find out?'

'When that daughter of his came visiting him on the weekend.'

'Well, why shouldn't she visit him? He's her father!'

'I knew that girl and her family would be a bad influence on you,' said his mother.

'That girl?' shouted Matthew. 'That girl's my friend! She's the best friend I've ever had! You've never liked her just because she's black! And because her family's poor, and they don't drive round in an expensive car! It's not her fault her father's in prison. And she's not a thief!' Matthew couldn't hold back the tears. 'Well, I'd rather live with her family than with you!' He ran out of the house.

Matthew headed along the road towards town, walking fast, trying to get his feelings under control. At first, he couldn't even think. After a little while, he became calmer, and started to think about the argument he'd just had with his parents. He knew he shouldn't have shouted at them like that. But he didn't care, he didn't care! He'd meant what he said. Oh, he loved his mother and father all right, and he really didn't want to hurt their feelings. But he'd changed! He was no longer the same person he'd been when they moved up here from Perth. And he knew why. In a way his mother was right – it was because of Noname and her family. They had opened up a different view of life for him. It was as if he had been waiting for this to happen. It wasn't just the hunting, the excitement of learning new things, though that was part of it. More important was the feeling of being so at home when he was with his new friends. It was quite different from anything he'd known. He didn't care who

No-name's father was, or what he had done.

He tried to understand his own feelings. Why did he like No-name's family so much? Partly, it was the way people behaved with one another. They seemed so easygoing and accepting of other people – of him. And they were not interested in having things, making money, being busy. They didn't worry about how they looked. They seemed to take life as it came, to just get on with it. He knew they weren't *saints*. But they seemed to have a different idea of what was important in life, one that made sense to Matthew.

Matthew kept walking and thinking, thinking about the future. He knew he couldn't stay behind if his parents went to Perth. They would never allow it. And in any case, he had nowhere to stay. All his family lived down south, and he couldn't really stay with No-name's family. He would have to go to Perth, that he knew. He would have to complete his schooling there. But no one could keep him in Perth forever, no one. Once he had finished school, he would be free. And he would come back. 'I'll come back,' he said aloud. 'Whatever else happens to me, as long as I'm alive, I promise I'll come back.'

Once he had made this decision, Matthew felt calmer. After a while he turned and started to head home. By the time he reached his front door he was ready to *apologise* to his parents.

'Look, I'm sorry I got angry,' he said. 'I know I have to go to Perth with you. I don't want to leave here, but I know if you go, I have to go as well. I just wasn't expecting it so soon.'

saint, extremely good and unselfish person
apologise, say one is sorry for having done something wrong

His parents listened without answering, still angry with Matthew for the things he had said. He tried again.

'I didn't mean that about living with them rather than you,' he said, not sure if he was telling the truth. 'But I will miss them. Badly,' he added.

To avoid further discussion of No-name and her family, he went to his room. He lay on his bed looking up at the ceiling. He thought of all the places he knew, and imagined never seeing them again. He thought about the school, about Nick and his other friends. But the pictures that kept coming into his mind again and again were of No-name, her grandmother, and all the others in her family. They were the people he would miss the most.

Chapter 12 – I'll Come Back!

In those last few days before leaving, Matthew saw No-name as often as he could. He rode up to Two-mile each day after school, and she was usually somewhere around, waiting for him. Sometimes he just sat with No-name and her grandmother and whoever else was at their house. Other times, Matthew and No-name went for a walk in the nearby bush, looking for tracks. Once they went as far as Limestone *Quarry*, just outside the town. They climbed over the rocks, then sat still and watched the birds and other wildlife.

quarry, ['kwɒrɪ] place where rocks, sand, etc. are dug out of the ground

Towards sunset, they climbed to the very top of the rocks, and stood together looking down at the town below. Matthew knew this was the last time he would see this view for a very long time. Perhaps forever.

'I'll come back, No-name,' he said suddenly, without looking at her. 'I promise you, I'll come back!' No-name's hand touched his and fell again, but she didn't speak.

Most of Matthew's school friends seemed to think he was lucky to be going to Perth. They couldn't understand why he wasn't happy about it. He didn't try to explain. He had kept his friendship with No-name and her family pretty much to himself. He felt that it would be treated by some of the others as a bit of a joke. He liked to keep the time they spent together as something special between them. Only Nick understood what it meant to him.

'You're going to miss all this,' Nick said one day.

'That's for sure,' said Matthew, happy that at least someone realised how he felt. 'Everyone else seems to think I should be glad to go back to Perth.'

'That's because they like doing different kinds of things. You've got into the life up here in a way none of the rest of us has. You've made real friends with the locals. It'll be hard to get used to life in the city. But don't take it too hard. I think you'll be back.'

'You think so?' Matthew looked at Nick hopefully.

'Nothing is surer!'

On the morning they were leaving, Matthew's father was up at sunrise, loading the last of the family's belongings into the car. His mother was rushing around cleaning. Matthew cleared his room and put the last things in his backpack for the trip. In the front pocket he found the pair of fire-making sticks No-name had given him at their first meeting. He had never managed to make a fire with them. As he looked at the sticks again, he realised they were the only reminder he would have of No-name. He tied the sticks together and put them back in his backpack. Then there was nothing else for him to do but have breakfast. He found he couldn't eat, and left the table to sit on the front step. His eyes were fixed on the road that led to town, and beyond town to Two-mile, but it was empty.

At last everything was ready to go. Matthew's mother and father were already in the front seats of the car. Matthew opened the door and climbed in next to the bags and boxes piled on one side of the back seat. His father started the engine. They were just pulling out onto the road, when the familiar old brown truck appeared suddenly at the bend in the road.

'Wait!' Matthew shouted. 'It's Frances!' His father said nothing, but he stopped the car.

As usual, there were people leaning out of both windows and sitting on the back. Matthew jumped out of his father's car and went up to the truck. He put out his hand and touched No-name's arm. He greeted the other people in the truck. No-name's grandmother smiled at Matthew and he shook her hand. He could not speak.

No-name climbed down from the truck and stood beside it, looking at the ground. Matthew took her hand and held it for a moment, not daring to look at her. Then, turning away his face, he climbed back into the car. Both his parents waved at the people in the old truck, then his father started off.

Matthew sat leaning out of the window, looking behind, waving. He was thankful that his parents did not speak. The truck was still standing outside the house in which he had lived. He watched No-name get smaller and smaller. The tears Matthew had been holding back now ran down his face.

'I'll come back, No-name!' he said aloud. 'I'll come back one day, I promise!'

The car drove around a bend, and Matthew carried away with him his last image of No-name, a tiny dark figure in the morning light.

Questions

Chapter 1 - Lost

1. Why does Matthew want to go camping at Goanna Gorge?
2. Describe the rock paintings Matthew discovers.
3. What does Matthew think might happen if he discovers more paintings? Why does he think he should keep the paintings a secret?
4. How does Matthew get lost? What mistakes does he make?

Chapter 2 - Found

1. What would happen if Matthew didn't come home the next day?
2. How does the girl know that Matthew has spent the night in the bush?
3. How does the girl try to make a fire? Does she succeed?
4. Why does the girl not have a name?

Chapter 3 - No-name

1. Why is No-name's grandmother not surprised to see Matthew?
2. Where do No-name and her grandmother live?
3. Why do No-name and her grandmother laugh at the idea of getting lost in the bush?
4. Why has Matthew never been inside a 'community'?

Chapter 4 - Home

1. Why does Matthew feel he has to tell his parents what happened at Goanna Gorge?
2. How do Matthew's parents react when he tells them about No-name?
3. When Matthew's mother says they could give No-name a present, Matthew's father says, 'If she hasn't got one already.' What do you think he means?
4. What does Matthew decide to do as he lies in bed thinking about his adventure that night?

Chapter 5 - No-name Again

1. How do the police find Matthew's missing backpack and sleeping-bag?
2. In what way is No-name different at the police station from out in the bush?
3. What do Matthew's parents think happened to his belongings?
4. Why is Matthew sure that No-name didn't steal his things?

Chapter 6 - A Mystery Solved

1. Whom does Matthew meet at the Two-mile community?
2. What is No-name doing at Matthew's school?
3. Who took Matthew's backpack and sleeping-bag?
4. Why didn't No-name return the things to Matthew straight away?

Chapter 7 - Jampijin

1. What do you think Matthew's father means when he says, 'You'll learn the hard way'?
2. What is 'Jampijin'? What does Matthew think of being Jampijin?
3. How often do No-name and her family go camping in the bush?
4. What happens at four o'clock on Friday afternoon? What does Matthew's father say?

Chapter 8 - Back to the Bush

1. Who are the people Matthew meets in the old truck?
2. Where is No-name's father? Why doesn't he have a job any more?
3. What are bush coconuts? What does Matthew think of them?
4. Why did No-name's family not pick up Matthew the day before?

Chapter 9 - Emu in the Sky

1. What animals does No-name find in a hole under a tree? How does she know they are there?
2. What is the emu in the sky?
3. What animal does No-name hunt down and kill? What does Matthew want to do with it?
4. Why does Matthew not bring his 'little Aboriginal friend' home with him?

Chapter 10 - Surprise Meeting

1. Why does Matthew ride to school with his father?
2. Who helps Matthew's father out?
3. What does Matthew's father say about the young men?

Chapter 11 - A Shock

1. What shocking news do Matthew's parents tell him?
2. What does Matthew's father know about No-name's family?
3. What does Matthew decide to do in the future?

Chapter 12 - I'll Come Back!

1. Why do Matthew's friends think he is lucky to move to Perth? Who is the only one who understands him?
2. What does Matthew find in the front pocket of his backpack?
3. Do you think Matthew will come back one day? Write a new chapter in which Matthew comes back from Perth to visit No-name.

Activities

1. True or false. Which of the following sentences about the story are true and which are false?
   a. Matthew decides to camp at Goanna Gorge because he wants to look for Aboriginal rock paintings.
   b. The Aboriginal girl Matthew meets at Goanna Gorge has no name because her parents forgot to give her one.
   c. No-name's grandmother has a house in the community called Two-mile.
   d. Matthew's parents don't care that his sleeping-bag and backpack have been stolen.
   e. The police sergeant tells Matthew that he cannot trust the Aboriginal people.
   f. No-name does not tell the police that Alfie took Matthew's belongings because she is afraid they would put him in prison.
   g. The man who drives the old truck to the camp is No-name's father.
   h. No-name shows Matthew a constellation that looks like a big dingo in the sky.
   i. When Matthew's father's car runs out of petrol, Alfie and his friends help him out.
   j. Matthew's friends think that Matthew is very unlucky to be moving to Perth.

2. Use the following words to fill in the blanks in the sentences below. Then use the words in sentences of your own.

ashamed	hungry
curious	puzzled
disappointed	rude
embarrassed	sensible
frightened	shy

a. When our father told us we weren't allowed to camp at Goanna Gorge, we were quite ________.
b. I was very ________ of the snake, but my father told me it wasn't dangerous.
c. When my mother kissed me in front of my school friends, I was so ________!
d. He was ________ about Aboriginal customs and decided to borrow a book about them from the library.
e. Any ________ person would bring a water-bottle when going into the desert.
f. She didn't want to be ________, so she waited for everyone else to finish eating before she left the table.
g. When his parents found out he had stolen the backpack, he felt very ________ of what he had done.
h. I'm sorry, but after you told me we're having goanna for dinner, I'm not ________ any more.
i. I was very ________. How could the girl possibly know which way the snake was going?
j. When the police sergeant asked the little boy if he was lost, the boy was too ________ to answer.

apologise	remind
blame	spoil
dare	steal
examine	tease
hesitate	trust

a If I told my friends that I don't know how to ride a bicycle, they would ________ me about it.
b. The teacher told her to ________ to the boy for calling him a thief.
c. I stopped to ________ the tracks and saw that they had been made by a dingo puppy.
d. When my sister's bicycle was stolen, I knew she would ________ me for not locking it.
e. If you can't find the book you need, don't ________ to ask the librarian for help.
f. He told me I shouldn't ________ someone who has just got out of prison.
g. Will you ________ me to buy petrol on the way back from town?
h. I don't think I would ________ to pick up a dingo puppy if its mother was nearby.
i. He told the police sergeant he didn't ________ the wallet, he was only borrowing it.
j. If you knew what bush coconuts were, it might ________ your appetite, so I'd better not tell you.

aunt	reporter
cousin	saint
drunk	thief
explorer	trespasser
librarian	wimp

a. Last night a ________ stole our car and left it at the quarry.
b. This is my ________ Josephine, who is married to my uncle Bob.
c. A famous British ________ named this gorge Goanna Gorge in 1837.
d. He is no ________, so don't ask him to hold your wallet while you go play basketball.
e. She is my ________, the daughter of my father's sister.
f. The police sergeant arrested a ________ who had started a fight in a bar.
g. I didn't realise I was talking to a ________ until I read her article in the newspaper.
h. He's such a ________! He's afraid of falling off his bicycle!
i. How embarrassing! The ________ asked me to return the book I borrowed a year ago.
j. If you climb over that fence, they might think you are a ________ and fine you.

3. At one point in the story, Matthew's mother says, 'We're not racist or anything, but, well, people are usually much better off if they stick with their own kind.' Why do you think Matthew's parents react the way they do when they hear about Matthew's new friend? Do you think they are racist? How do the white people and Aboriginal people in the book feel about each other? Are there similar problems in your country? What can be done to improve relations between people?

Find more excercises on
www.easyreaders.eu

EASY READERS *Denmark*
ERNST KLETT SPRACHEN *Germany*
ARCOBALENO *Spain*
PRACTICUM EDUCATIEF BV. *Holland*
EUROPEAN SCHOOLBOOKS PUBLISHING LTD. *UK and Eire*
EMC CORP. *USA*

This edition has been abridged and simplified to provide graduated reading exercises for students of English. Vocabulary and sentence structures have been selected because of their high frequency and practical value to the learner.
Words which are difficult to understand in context or fall out of the EASY READER frequency modules are explained by footnotes in simple English or by illustrations.
EASY READERS are suitable for use in schools, for home study, or simply for reading enjoyment. See the complete list of titles on the inside cover.
EASY READERS are also available in German, French, Spanish, Italian and Russian.

EASY READER TITLES NOW AVAILABLE:
Sir Arthur Conan Doyle: The Red Circle (A)
Sir Arthur Conan Doyle: The Speckled Band (A)
Lois Lowry: Number the Stars (A)
R. L. Stine: Stay Out of the Basement (A)
R. L. Stevenson: The Bottle Imp (A)
Oscar Wilde: The Canterville Ghost (A)
Enid Blyton: Five on a Treasure Island (B)
Roald Dahl: The Way up to Heaven and Other Stories (B)
Sir Arthur Conan Doyle: Black Peter - The Red-Headed League (B)
Lois Duncan: I know what you did last Summer (B)
Lois Duncan: Killing Mr. Griffin (B)
Colin Higgins: Harold and Maude (B)
S.E. Hinton: The Outsiders (B)
Jerome K. Jerome: Three Men in a Boat (B)
Ira Levin: The Stepford Wives (B)
Pat Lowe: The Girl with No Name (B)
R. L. Stine: Fear Street: The Perfect Date (B)
Mark Twain: Tom Sawyer (B)
Oscar Wilde: The Happy Prince (B)
Richard Wright: Black Boy (B)
Karen Blixen: Out of Africa (C)
Tim Bowler: Storm Catchers (C)
Sir Arthur Conan Doyle: The Hound of the Baskervilles (C)
Graham Greene: The Third Man (C)
Ernest Hemingway: The Snows of Kilimanjaro and Other Stories (C)
James Heneghan: Safe House (C)
S.E. Hinton: Tex (C)
Ira Levin: Rosemary's Baby (C)
James Moloney: Gracey (C)
Mary Shelley: Frankenstein (C)
Alexander McCall Smith: Tears of the Giraffe (C)
R. L. Stevenson: Treasure Island (C)
Bram Stoker: Dracula (C)
Oscar Wilde: The Picture of Dorian Gray (C)
F. Scott Fitzgerald: The Great Gatsby (D)
Alan Sillitoe: The Loneliness of the Long Distance Runner (D)
R. L. Stevenson: Dr. Jekyll and Mr. Hyde (D)
Kurt Vonnegut: Slaughterhouse-Five (D)

ADULT:
Peter James: The Perfect Murder (B)
Stephen Speight: Doomed to Die (B)
Minette Walters: Chickenfeed (C)